OUTSIDE AND INSIDE
DINOSAURS

BY SANDRA MARKLE

ALADDIN PAPERBACKS

New York London Toronto Sydney Singapore

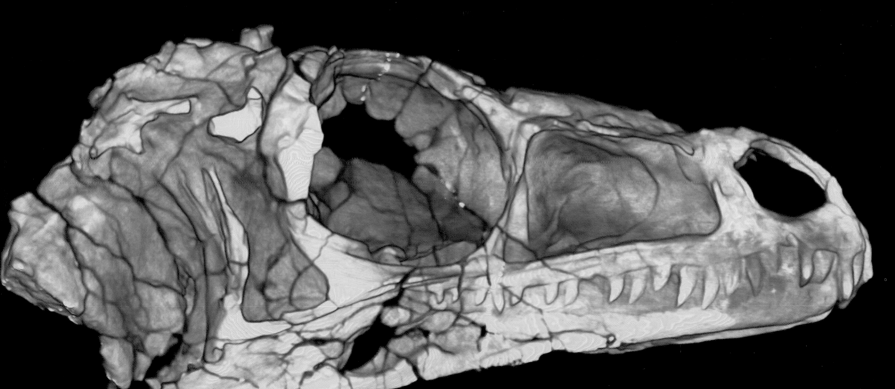

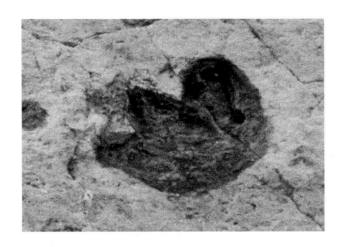

AUTHOR'S NOTE

There were lots of different kinds of *dinosaurs* that lived in different eras, across a very long span of time in Earth's ancient past. The parts they left behind when they died are called *fossils*.

There are two kinds of dinosaur fossils: body fossils and trace fossils. Body fossils look like bones but they are really stone. They formed when dinosaur bodies were buried. The soft parts decomposed and the hard bones that remained were slowly replaced by minerals. You can see these kinds of minerals by setting out a pan of water for a few days. The water disappears, leaving a crusty material behind that contains the minerals that were in the water.

Trace fossils are dinosaur droppings or eggs that were replaced by stone, just like body fossils. Other kinds of trace fossils are imprints of skin or body parts and footprints like the one above stamped into mud and sand that later hardened into rock.

The last living dinosaur died millions of years ago and the only way people can learn about them today is by studying fossils—the remains of bones, eggs, droppings, skin, and footprints.

So what did dinosaurs look like when they were alive? How did their bodies work? How did they behave?

While these questions may never be answered fully, people keep finding new ways to use technology to reveal clues about the dinosaurs. In this book, you'll explore these prehistoric creatures and see what science is uncovering. What you discover may surprise you!

Look at the X ray of a living alligator's bones and a dinosaur's *skeleton*. In the process of becoming fossils, the dinosaur's skeleton fell apart into a pile of bones. To put the skeleton together, researchers study the bony framework of similar living animals like alligators.

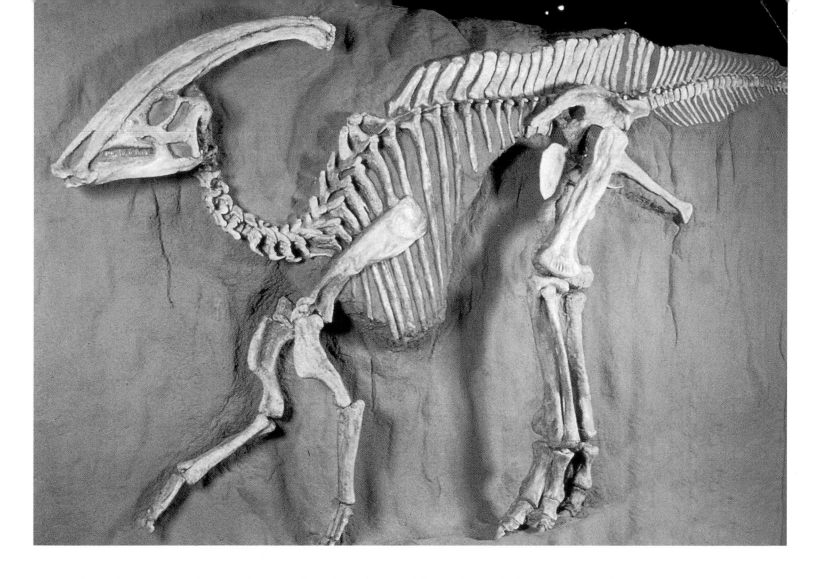

The dinosaur's skeleton looks a lot like the alligator's. Alligators are reptiles, and dinosaurs are thought of as a group of reptiles that is now completely gone from the earth. One big difference between dinosaurs and most living reptiles is their legs. See how the alligator sprawls with its legs out to its sides? That's typical of today's reptiles, and it's why an alligator's body swings from side-to-side as it walks.

So if an alligator's legs are at its sides, why did experts put the dinosaur skeleton together with its legs straight under its body?

Take a close look at these dinosaur footprints. They show that the dinosaur traveling along the path marked by the string walked straight ahead—the way *you* walk. Experts decided a dinosaur's legs were probably straight under its body the way yours are. What are some other things you can discover about a dinosaur by looking at its tracks?

You can tell if it walked on two legs or four legs and if it was big or little. You can also learn if the dinosaur was walking or running. Just like you, a running dinosaur took longer steps than one that was walking. So a running dinosaur's footprints are farther apart.

Now, look at this *Allosaurus*' foot. Like your foot, it is made up of a lot of small bones. Take a couple of steps barefoot while watching your feet move. A body can only bend where two bones meet so seeing the structure of a dinosaur's foot can also reveal some secrets about how it walked and ran.

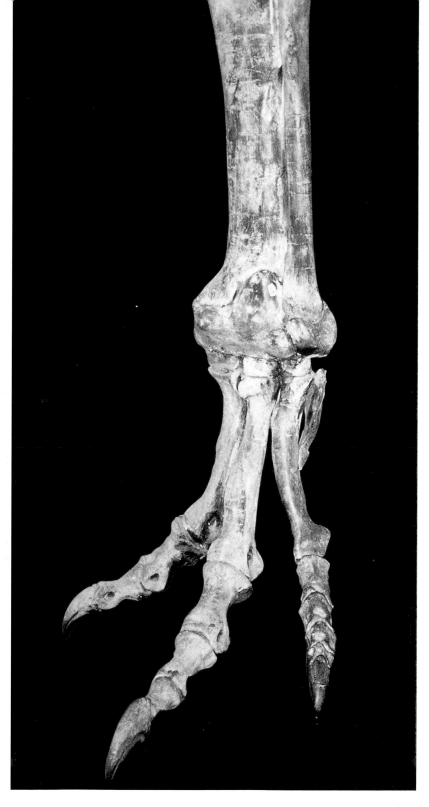

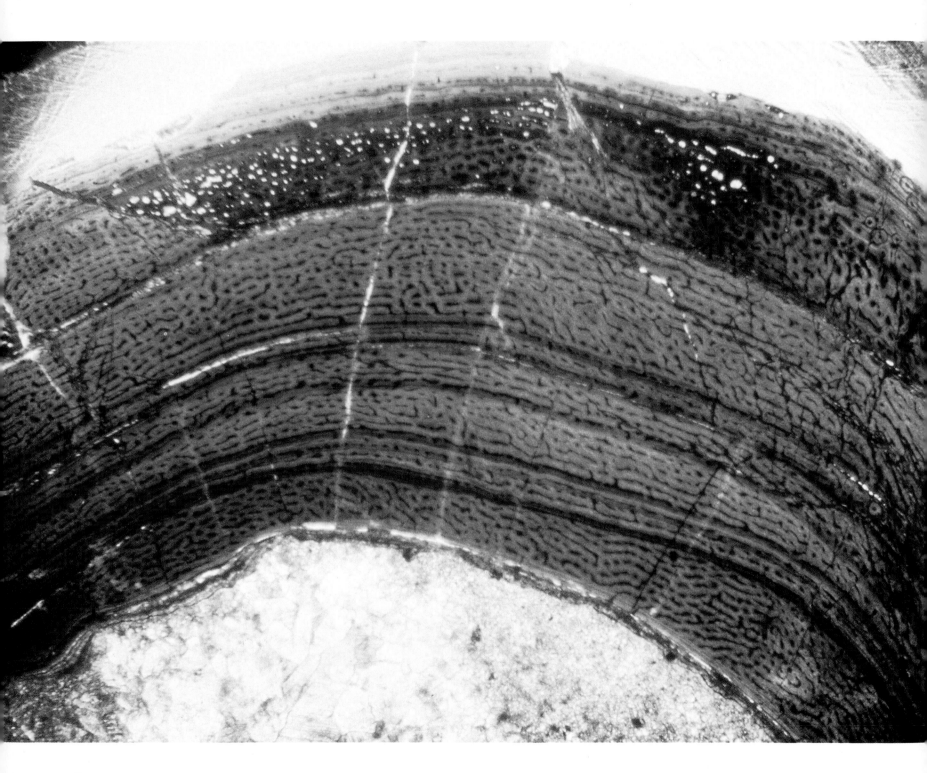

A special tool, called a *microscope,* was used to enlarge this slice of a *Troödon's* leg bone. It offers a clue to solving a mystery: Did dinosaurs produce their own body heat or did they just soak up heat from the world around them?

See the rings in the bone? Some dinosaur experts believe these rings could mean the dinosaur soaked up heat. All animals need heat energy to be active and grow, so the dinosaur may have grown more when it was warmer. However not all dinosaur bones have rings. Some dinosaur bones are full of holes, like the bones of animals that make their own body heat. When the dinosaur was alive, the holes were filled with tubes that carried blood. The blood quickly spread heat energy throughout the animal's body.

But the question still remains: Did dinosaurs produce their own heat? More clues are needed to solve this mystery.

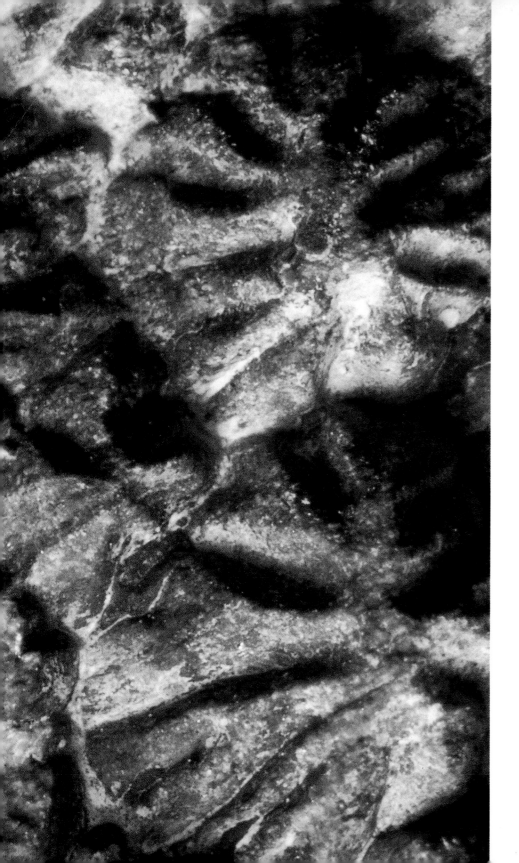

Here's another clue. It's an imprint of a *Hadrosaurus'* skin. The little bumps are like those on an alligator. This sort of scaly skin is a good, tough covering for a body that soaks up heat by lying on the ground. So did all dinosaurs have scaly skin?

POSSIBLE FEATHERY SCALES

Dinosaur imprints, like this one of a *Sinosauropteryx,* make some researchers believe there were dinosaurs with feathery scales. If these were like down feathers they would have been good for holding in body heat. Feathered scales could be proof that at least *some* dinosaurs produced their own heat.

Other researchers don't think such imprints show skin at all. Some believe the imprints show frilly fins like those seen on the backs of some of today's lizards. Others believe the imprints show a kind of tissue that lies just underneath the skin, connecting the skin to the muscles and bones.

This computer image lets you peek inside a fossil *Syntarsus* skull. Experts wondered if dinosaurs had sinuses, spaces inside the skull to warm up air as it was breathed in. Present day animals that produce their own body heat usually have sinuses. So do you.

To keep from destroying rare fossils by slicing them open, researchers used X-rays to create a picture of the spaces inside. First, they passed X-rays through the skull from several different directions. Then a computer assembled the X-ray images and color enhanced them to create a 3-D model of the inside of the dinosaur's skull.

Experts did discover sinuses inside the dinosaur's skull, but they learned something else. The dinosaurs they studied only had a small space for a brain. Today's animals that produce their own heat usually have large brains. That lets them be quick and clever enough to catch lots of food. Producing heat takes lots of food energy. Of course, it's possible giant dinosaurs didn't need to be smart or fast to catch enough food to eat.

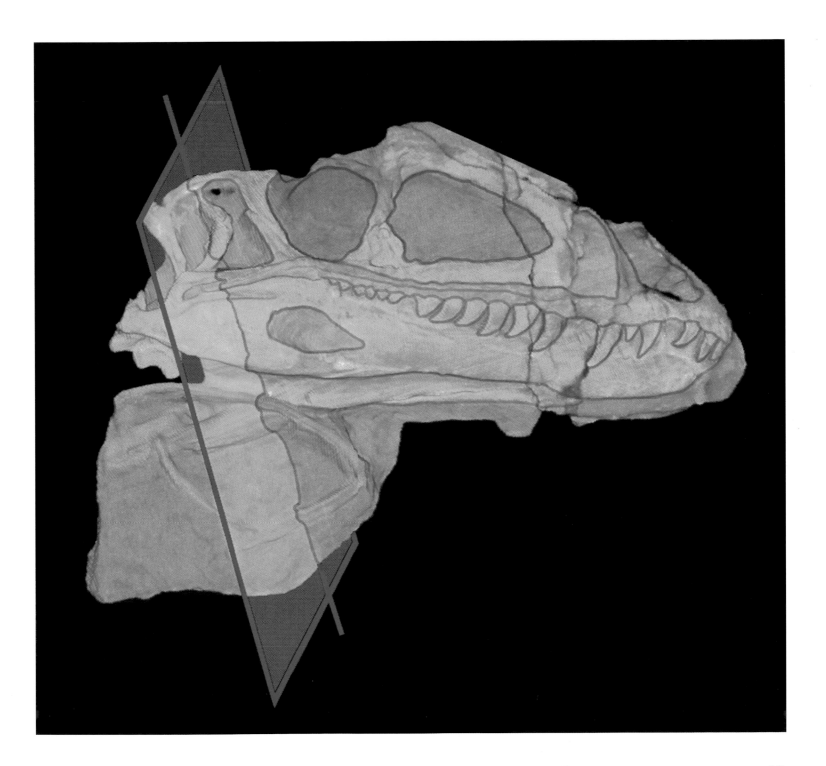

Check out this *Parasaurolophus* skull. Why do you think that dinosaur needed such a long crest?

That was a mystery some scientists wanted to solve. So they used the same X-ray process that was used to check for sinuses, to peek inside the dinosaur's crest. What they discovered were lots of empty spaces. They wondered if the spaces helped the dinosaur make sounds.

A model was built of the airflow inside the crest using plastic tubing. When air was blown through this model, it made a trumpetlike sound.

Imagine a whole heard of trumpeting dinosaurs! Since some Parasaurolophus skulls have longer crests than others, each dinosaur probably had its own special voice.

Can you guess what this is? It's part of something else dinosaurs left behind—droppings. Of course, just like other dinosaur fossils, the soft, stinky material was replaced by minerals. Scientists are studying dinosaur droppings to help solve yet another mystery: What did dinosaurs eat?

Check out these microscopic views of droppings from two different dinosaurs. Can you tell which one ate meat?

You're right if you guessed the one on the top. Look closely and you'll see pieces of animal bone. The long slivers in the fossil on the bottom are wood fibers, proof that those are droppings from a plant-eating dinosaur.

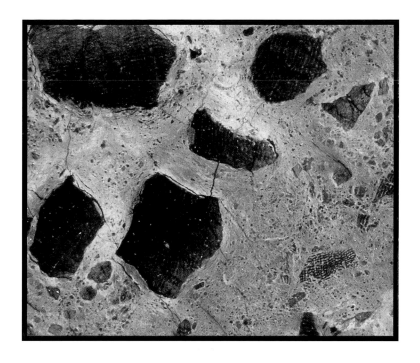

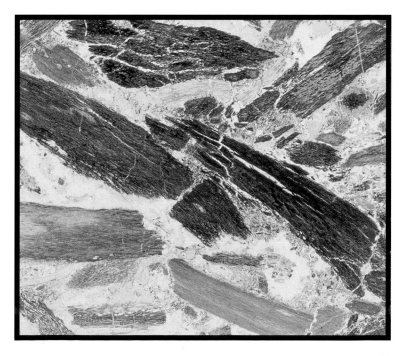

18

Dinosaurs' teeth can also be a clue to what they ate.

You probably guessed that a big, sharp tooth like this belonged to a meat-eater. In fact, it belonged to *Tyrannosaurus rex,* one of the biggest meat-eating dinosaurs.

Researchers wondered if the T. rex hunted living prey or if it just ate what it found dead. When a fossil bone was found with centimeter (half-inch) deep T. rex tooth marks on it, one scientist decided to try an experiment.

With the help of an engineer, he built and tested a model of a T. rex tooth. This was made of aluminum and bronze to be as strong as a real tooth. Next, the tooth was driven into cow bone to make a bite as deep as the one on the fossil bone. Then the force needed to bite that deeply was computed. This proved that T. rex's bite was more powerful than an alligator's or a great white shark's—surely strong enough for the dinosaur to kill its prey.

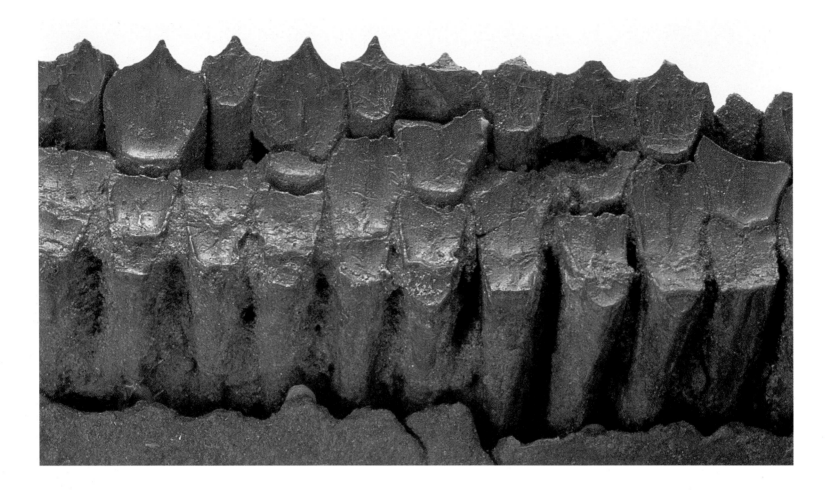

Now, look at these Hadrosaurus teeth. You probably guessed these batches of flattened teeth belonged to a plant-eater. Studies of Hadrosaurus jawbones also showed new teeth formed in pockets below the old ones. Experts guess these moved up to replace any lost teeth.

Two scientists created a computer program called DinoMorph to solve another dinosaur mystery: Did *Apatosaurus'* really long neck let it munch leaves in treetops? If your neck was as long as this dinosaur's, you could stand on the ground and peek into a sixth floor window!

The DinoMorph program showed the neck bones probably locked if the dinosaur lifted its head higher than its back. The scientists now wonder if its long neck let Apatosaurus eat plants that were all around it before walking forward to find more food.

STONES

Look at all the little stones near *Caudipteryx*'s rib bones. Researchers think the dinosaur swallowed these stones on purpose. Can you guess why it may have done that?

Look at all the grit inside this bird's gizzard. Again, studying living animals can reveal clues about dinosaurs. Birds swallow grit and even pebbles on purpose to help grind up their food. Dinosaurs probably did the same thing.

To see how stones and grit help, put some rocks and lettuce leaves into an empty container with a snap-on lid and shake ten times. You'll find the lettuce leaves are crushed and broken.

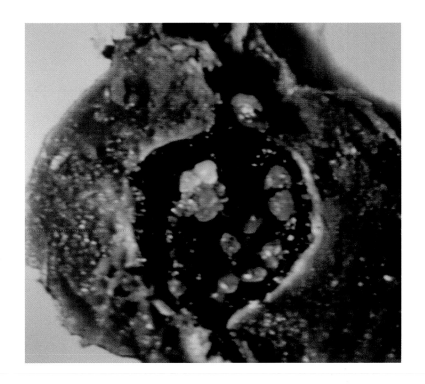

Now, take a close look at something really amazing—a dinosaur's guts! Soft body parts usually rot away as a fossil forms so researchers were excited when they saw this dinosaur fossil. It showed the intestine, liver, and even part of the wind pipe of this baby *Scipionyx,* a meat-eating cousin of T. rex. Seeing these body parts showed dinosaur digestion probably happened the same way it does in present day animals.

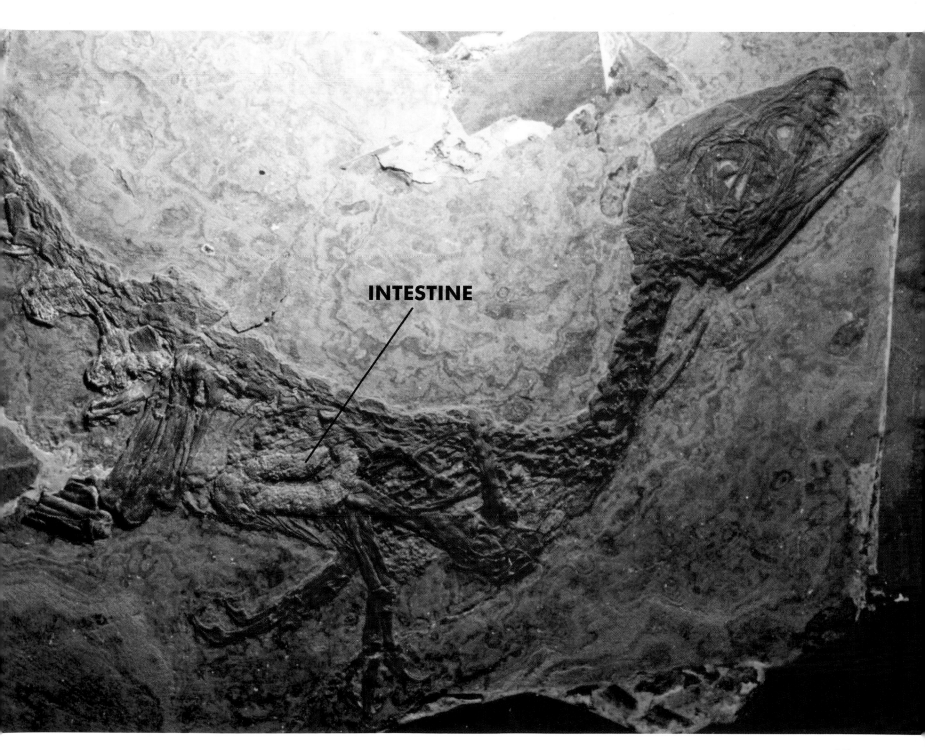

INTESTINE

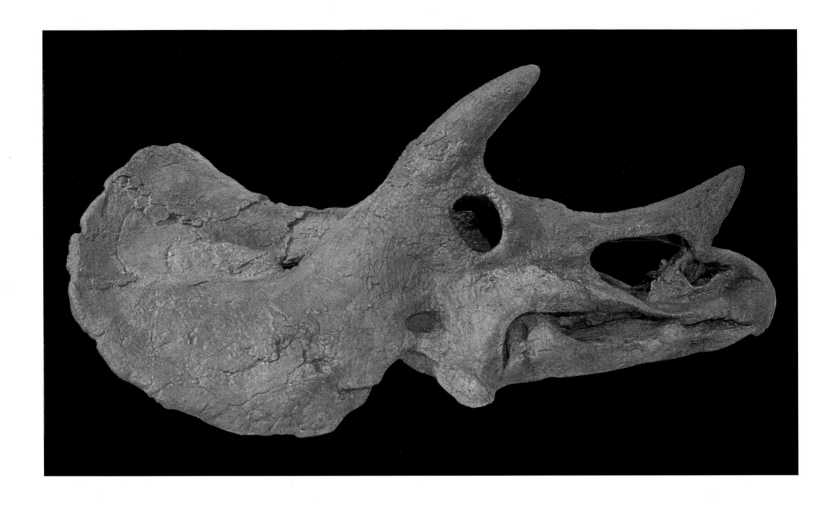

This is a *Triceratops* skull. It got its name from the three horns on its head, though you can only see two here.

Experts think Triceratops was a slow-moving plant-eater. The horns probably helped protect it from meat-eating dinosaurs. The horns could have helped Triceratops in another way. Some had bigger horns than others. Like the antlers of present day deer, these could have helped attract a mate.

Did you guess this fossil was a claw? It belonged to *Deinonychus.* That dinosaur had a large, curved claw on the second toe of each hind foot. Dinosaur experts believe this toe was held up and back until Deinonychus attacked. Then it jerked forward, slashing the prey. Because several skeletons for Deinonychus have been found together, researchers think these dinosaurs may have hunted in packs, the way some animals, like wolves, hunt today.

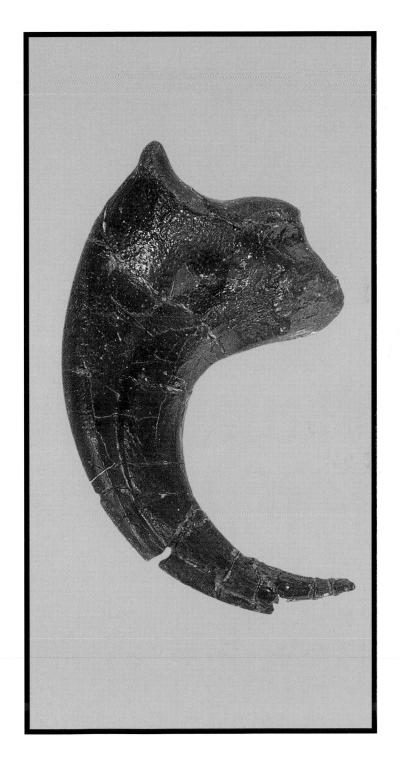

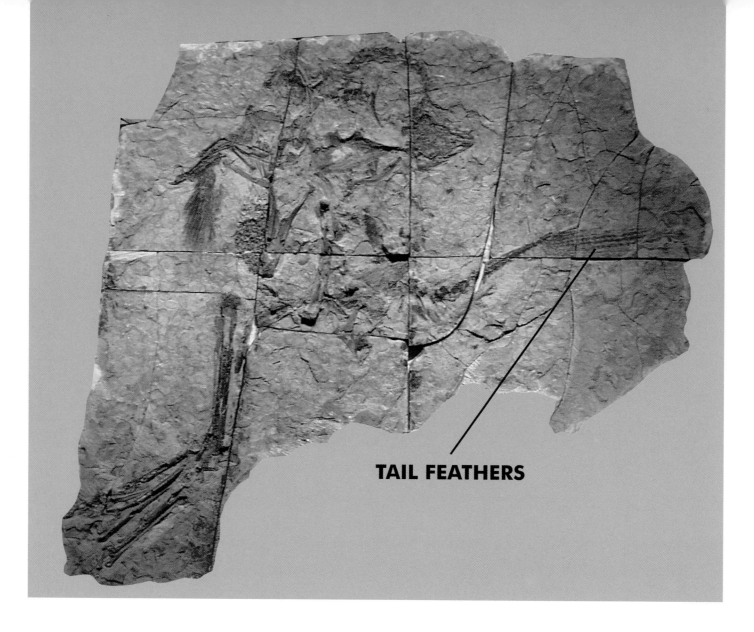

TAIL FEATHERS

Take a close look at the imprint of Caudipteryx again. Maybe it didn't just have feathery scales like Sinosauropteryx. Maybe it had feathers. Investigating feathered dinosaurs leads researchers to wonder about one of the biggest dinosaur mysteries of all: Were feathered dinosaurs able to fly?

In order to figure out what features dinosaurs would have needed for flight, one researcher studied how birds fly today.

He recorded movies of birds in flight. He also connected tiny instruments to a bird's body to measure muscle activity during a single wingbeat.

What he discovered was that some dinosaurs did have some features that would let them fly. For example, they had special joints that allowed the upper limbs to twist and turn for wing strokes. But the dinosaur fossils that were studied didn't have the shoulder structure that birds have to make the rapid upstrokes needed for flight. Of course, other experts point out it's possible that feathered dinosaurs were not really dinosaurs. Or maybe they just flew differently than today's birds.

Scientists have discovered fossil dinosaur eggs—some filled with rock containing skeletons of baby dinosaurs. Like birds' eggs today, dinosaur eggs appear to have had a hard shell full of pores or holes. These probably let oxygen in and carbon dioxide out. This exchange of gases would have supported the baby dinosaur growing inside.

Each kind of dinosaur laid its own unique kind of egg. Some dinosaur eggs are round. Others are pointed on one end. Still others, like these T. rex eggs, are long ovals. The bigger the dinosaur, the bigger the eggs. Some kinds of dinosaurs laid eggs no more than 2.5 centimeters (an inch) long. Others, like T. rex, laid eggs as big as 45 centimeters (18 inches) long.

Look how much bigger the T. rex eggs are than the fossil bird egg! And that bird's egg was much bigger than present day chicken eggs.

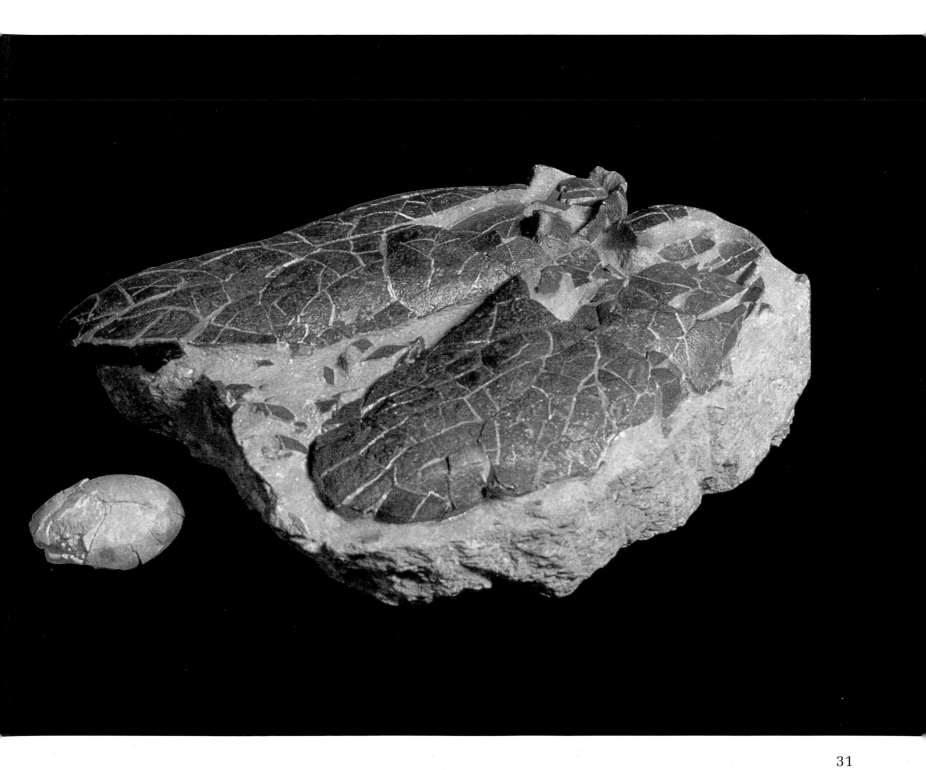

The eggs of some dinosaurs, like these Troödon eggs, have been found in hollow pit nests. That makes experts wonder about yet another mystery: Did dinosaur parents keep their eggs warm the way birds do? The answer may have been different for different types of dinosaurs. One scientist reported Troödons probably did. He found carbon left over from ancient plant matter only around the lower part of the eggs. He believed that showed Troödon parents crouched over the top of their eggs to warm them.

Check out this colony of nesting penguins! Like birds that nest in colonies today, dinosaurs may have nested together to let the parents share in protecting the eggs from enemies. At Egg Mountain in Choteau, Montana, there is a whole area full of *Orodromeus* dinosaur nests. Groups of dinosaur nests have been found in other parts of the world too.

This dinosaur baby was found inside its egg. It's a rare find. It's also an important clue to a dinosaur mystery: How did baby dinosaurs change as they developed?

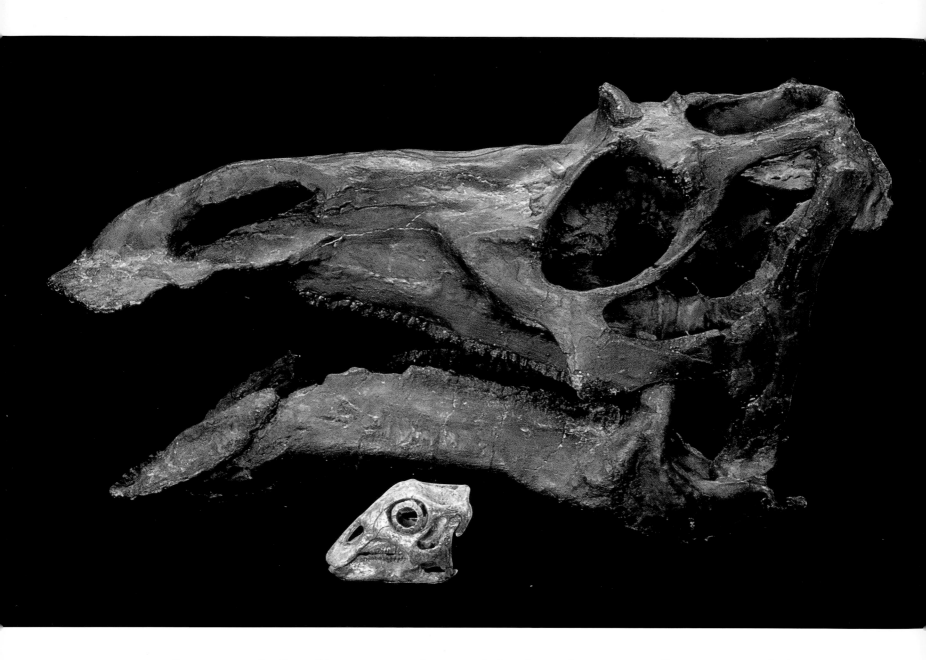

One way baby dinosaurs changed is that they grew bigger. Look how much bigger the adult *Maiasaura* skull is than the baby's. Think how much growing up the baby dinosaur had to do to become an adult!

Here's yet another clue about what dinosaurs were like: It's believed to be a sample of T. rex blood chemicals, recovered from a T. rex bone. Special tests and computers are being used to analyze these blood chemicals. Some researchers want to find out if they are really blood chemicals. Others wonder if they can use these chemicals to learn if the dinosaur was a male or a female.

As you can see, science and technology are uncovering new clues about dinosaurs. Many times those clues lead experts to think of even more mysteries to investigate.

Maybe some day you'll find new clues or develop new ways to use technology to solve the final mysteries of what dinosaurs were like—inside and out!

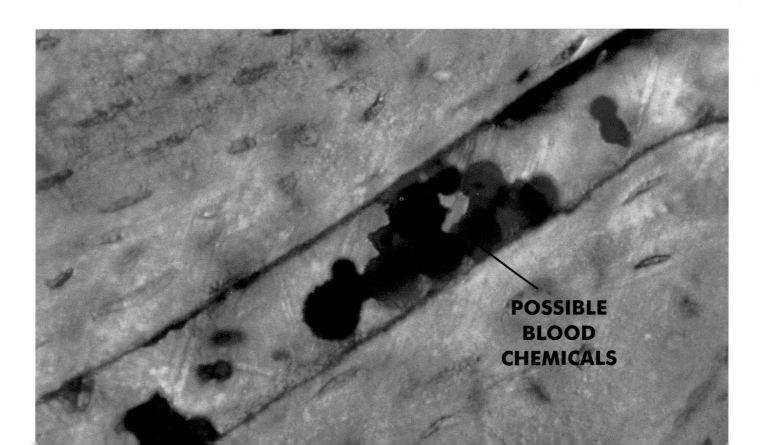

POSSIBLE
BLOOD
CHEMICALS

GLOSSARY/INDEX

NOTE: To help readers pronounce words that may not be familiar to them, pronounciations are given in the glossary/index. Glossary words are italicized the first time they appear.

ALLOSAURUS AL-oh-sawr-us: It walked on its hind legs and probably used its big tail to balance itself. **7**

APATOSAURUS uh-PAT-uh-SAWR-us: One of the biggest plant-eaters, it is also popularly known as *Brontosaurus*. **21**

CAUDIPTERYX caw-DIP-ter-iks: Its name means "tail feathers." This small dinosaur probably could not fly. **22, 28**

DEINONYCHUS die-NON-uh-kus: This dinosaur was thought to be a fast hunter that may have traveled in packs. It used its claws to slash its prey. **27**

DINOSAUR DIE-noh-sawr: A group of reptiles that is now completely gone from the earth. **2–7, 9–12, 15–17, 19, 21–24, 26–30, 34–37**

FOSSIL FAH-sil: The remains of living things. **2–4, 12, 16–17, 19, 24, 27, 30–31**

HADROSAURUS HAD-roh-SAWR-us: This big plant-eater had a spoon-shaped, duck-billed snout. **10, 20**

MAIASAURA MAY-yah-SAWR-ah: This dinosaur's name means "Good Mother Lizard." Its fossils were found among many dinosaur nests. **36**

MICROSCOPE MY-croh-scope: A tool used to magnify something. **9**

ORODROMEUS OR-oh-DROM-ee-us: A small plant-eater whose name means "egg mountain runner." **34**

PARASAUROLOPHUS PAR-ah-saw-ROL-oh-fus: Besides its crest, this dinosaur was also noted for its spoon-shaped, ducklike beak, and webbed front feet. **15**

SCIPIONYX SIP-ee-ON-iks: This baby dinosaur's fossil is the best look yet at a dinosaur's internal body parts. **24**

SINOSAUROPTERYX si-no-sawr-OP-ter-ix: It's name means "first Chinese dragon feather." It was named for imprints of downy-looking filaments some researchers believe are feather-like scales. It's believed to be a small meat-eater. **11, 28**

SKELETON SKEL-eh-ton: A body's bony framework. **4–5, 27**

SYNTARSUS sin-TAR-sus: This lightly-built meat-eater walked on its hind legs. Because of the fossil materials found, experts believe Syntarsus lived in a hot, desert climate. **12**

TRICERATOPS tri-SER-uh-tops: Noted for its three horns, it also has a big collar and a turtlelike beak. **26**

TROÖDON TRO-oh-don: Its tracks show this meat-eater was probably fast. It may also have hunted in packs. **9, 32**

TYRANNOSAURUS REX tye-RAN-oh-SAWR-us recks: Also called *T. rex*, this was one of the largest meat-eaters from the late dinosaur period. It was noted for its big jaws full of teeth. **19, 24, 30–31, 37**

ä as in c**a**rt   ā as in **a**pe   ə as in b**a**nan**a**   ē as in **e**ven   ī as in b**i**te

ō as in g**o**   ü as in r**u**le   ʉ as in f**u**r

DIGGING DEEPER

There are lots of places to see real dinosaur fossils for yourself. Here are a few:

DINOSAUR STATE PARK: The park in Rocky Hill, Connecticut, is home to one of the largest displays of dinosaur tracks—more than 500 in all. The trackways are covered by a dome to protect them from the weather.

AMERICAN MUSEUM OF NATURAL HISTORY: This New York City museum is famous for its displays of dinosaur fossils. They are set up as a time line. There are also displays that show how the dinosaurs may have looked and behaved.

WYOMING DINOSAUR CENTER: The center in Thermopolis, Wyoming, has quarries where lots of dinosaur fossils have been found. Here, visitors can watch researchers at work on a dinosaur "dig."

DINOSAUR NATIONAL MONUMENT: At the quarry located in Jensen, Utah, visitors see fossilized remains of more than two thousand bones.

DINOSAUR RIDGE: Located just west of Denver, Colorado, this is a great place to see lots of dinosaur tracks. There are also guided tours.

ROYAL TYRRELL MUSEUM: This museum is in Drumheller, Alberta, Canada. It offers visitors a chance to see beds of unassembled bones and assembled skeletons. There are also displays about finding and recovering dinosaur fossils.

PHOTO CREDITS

For my father Robert Haldeman, with love

The author would like to thank the following researchers for sharing their enthusiasm and expertise: Anthony Martin, John Horner, Tim Rowe, Karen Chin, Gregory Erickson, Michael Parrish, Kent Stevens, Spencer Lucas, Cambria Denison, Mary Scheitzer, Mark Marshall, and Terry Jones.

First Aladdin Paperbacks edition July 2003

ALADDIN PAPERBACKS
An imprint of Simon & Schuster
Children's Publishing Division
1230 Avenue of the Americas
New York, NY 10020

Also available in an Atheneum Books for Young Readers hardcover edition.
The text of this book was set in Melior.

Manufactured in China
2 4 6 8 10 9 7 5 3 1

The Library of Congress has cataloged the hardcover edition as follows:
Markle, Sandra.
Outside and inside dinosaurs / by Sandra Markle.—1st ed.
p. cm.
Includes index.
Summary: Describes the inner and outer workings of dinosaurs, discussing what
has been learned about their anatomy, diet, and behavior from fossils.
ISBN 0-689-82300-2
1. Dinosaurs—Juvenile literature. [1. Dinosaurs. 2. Fossils.] I. Title.
QE862.D5 .M356 2000   567.9—dc21   99-45808
ISBN 0-689-85778-0 (Aladdin pbk.)

Title page: 3-D reconstruction of *Eoraptor lunensis* by Cambria Denison, University of Texas (sample courtesy of Universidad Nacional de San Juan, Argentina, and Dr. Oscar Alcober)